To

I pray you'll grow to know
Jesus more and more and
to remember He loves you
so very much.

Love
Sherri

A Happy Day® Book Collection

Favorite Bible Stories

from the New Testament

Standard®
PUBLISHING

Cincinnati, Ohio

A Happy Day® Book Collection

Compilation copyright © 2010 by Standard Publishing

My Story of Jesus copyright © 2001, 2005 by Standard Publishing
Four Faithful Friends copyright © 1984, 2005 by Standard Publishing
Five Small Loaves and Two Small Fish copyright © 1992, 1996, 2005 by Standard Publishing
The Little Lost Sheep copyright © 1988, 1998, 2005 by Standard Publishing
Jesus Blesses the Children copyright © 2006 by Standard Publishing
Peter Said YES! copyright © 2009 by Standard Publishing
A Jailer Is Set Free copyright © 2006 by Standard Publishing
Paul's Great Adventures copyright © 2009 by Standard Publishing

Published by Standard Publishing, Cincinnati, Ohio, www.standardpub.com. Copyright © 2010 by Standard Publishing. All rights reserved. #05734. Manufactured in China, July 2010. No part of this book may be reproduced in any form, except for brief quotations in reviews, without the written permission of the publisher. Happy Day® is a registered trademark of Standard Publishing. Printed in: China. Project editor: Lu Ann J. Nickelson. Cover design: Sandra S. Wimmer. Inside design: Andrew Quach. Scripture taken from the *HOLY BIBLE, NEW INTERNATIONAL VERSION®. NIV®.* Copyright © 1973, 1978, 1984 by Biblica, Inc.™ Used by permission of Zondervan. All rights reserved.

ISBN   978-0-7847-2939-7

15 14 13 12 11 10   1 2 3 4 5 6 7 8 9

Contents

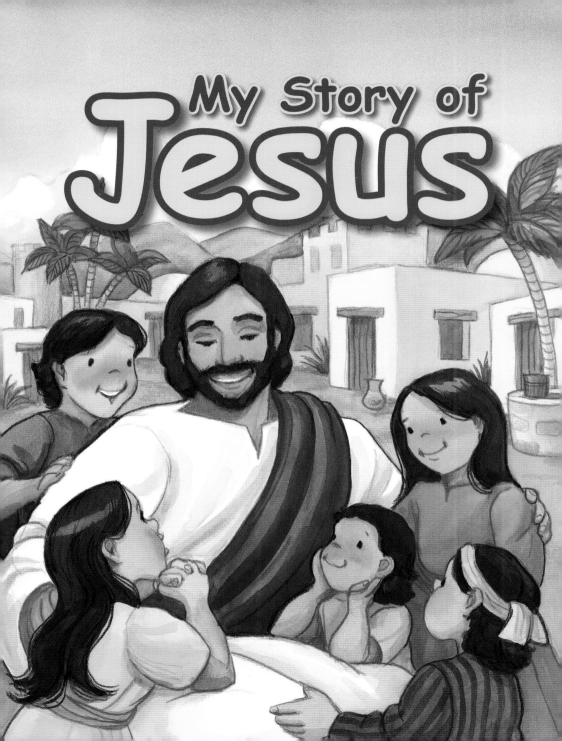

My Story of
Jesus

Long ago God said that he would send his Son to be the Savior and King of his people.

God's Son, Jesus, was born in Bethlehem. His mother, Mary, wrapped him in cloths and laid him in a manger.

As Jesus grew up, he obeyed his parents and pleased God. When he was 12, Jesus talked with the priests and teachers about God's teachings and God's love. They were amazed at how much Jesus understood.

A man named John was telling people about Jesus.
"Good news!" he said. "God has sent Jesus to save us.
We need to get ready for him!" People came to John to be
baptized.

Jesus came to be baptized too. When Jesus came up from the water, God's Spirit came from Heaven like a dove. Then a voice from Heaven said, "You are my Son. I love you. I am pleased with you."

Then Jesus began to do the work God had planned for him.

Jesus showed God's care and concern for people. He made sick people well and made blind people see again. He even made lame people able to walk!

11

Jesus showed God's power. One day when Jesus and some of his followers were in a boat, a terrible storm came up.

The followers were afraid, but Jesus told the wind and waves, "Quiet! Be still!" And the storm stopped.

13

Jesus became known as a wonderful teacher. Mothers and fathers brought their children to Jesus so he could bless them and pray for them. Jesus told stories to help people understand his teaching.

Jesus went to Jerusalem and ate the Passover meal with his followers. He told them he would leave them soon.

Then Jesus showed his followers a special way to always remember him. He gave thanks to God, broke bread, and passed it to his followers. He passed his cup to them too. "Remember me when you eat this bread and drink from this cup," said Jesus.

Jesus was ready to finish the work that God had planned for him. That meant he must die. This was part of God's plan for saving people from sin.

Jesus died on a cross. His followers were very sad. They buried Jesus' body in a tomb and closed it with a heavy stone.

But when some women went back to Jesus' tomb, they were surprised to find the stone was rolled away and the tomb was empty!

Suddenly, an angel appeared. "Jesus is not here," the angel told the women. "He is alive again!"

Many people saw Jesus after he had risen. Jesus told his followers, "Go everywhere and tell everyone the good news about me!"

Jesus returned to Heaven to make a new home for his
followers. But he promised to come back again one day.
What a happy day that will be!

There was a man who couldn't walk who wanted to see Jesus. He wanted Jesus to make him well. But how would he get to the house where Jesus was?

The man's friends talked it over. "No problem!" they said.

And they carried him on his mat to the house where Jesus was.

But when they got there, they couldn't get in. There was no room inside the house, no room outside the house, no room anywhere—*except* on the roof.

"No problem!" said the four friends. And they carried the man up to the roof.

But now they had a problem. How would they get the man into the house to see Jesus?

"No problem!" they said. And they made a hole in the roof.

The people in the house looked up. They saw the four friends and the man on his mat. How *would* the man get down?

"No problem," said the friends. Slowly, they lowered the man on his mat through the hole in the roof, into the house where Jesus was.

"Get up," said Jesus. "Take your mat and go home."

No one talked. No one moved. Could Jesus heal a man who couldn't walk?

"No problem!" said the man's four friends.

Everyone was amazed and filled with wonder when the man stood up and picked up his mat. "We haven't seen anything like this before!" they said.

And the man walked out the door and went home, praising God because Jesus had healed him.

On a hill, listening to Jesus, sat a boy. His stomach was growling. The boy had forgotten to eat his lunch.

Listening to Jesus was too wonderful to stop and eat.

But Jesus' disciples were getting worried. "It's getting late," they said to Jesus. "Send the people away so they can go and buy food."

"You can give them something to eat," said Jesus.
"How can we do that?" asked the disciples. "We don't
have enough money to buy food for all these people!"

But Jesus knew what he was going to do.
"How many loaves of bread do you have?"
Jesus asked. "Go and see."

One of the disciples, Andrew, found the hungry boy *and* the boy's lunch—five small loaves and two small fish.

"Please come with me to see Jesus," said Andrew. "And bring your lunch!"

Jesus smiled at the hungry boy.

"Tell the people to sit in groups," he said to his disciples.

Jesus thanked God for the food.

Then he broke the loaves and fish into pieces.

Everyone got some.

Everyone got as *much* as he could eat, *and* there was enough left over to fill twelve baskets.

"Jesus is someone special sent from God," the people said.

The boy was sure that they were right!

The Little Lost Sheep

Once there was a baby sheep who lived with his warm, woolly mother. They lived on a hill with lots of other warm, woolly sheep.

One spring morning the baby sheep decided to take a walk. He wanted to take a walk to see the world that God had made.

The baby sheep walked down the other side of the hill. He looked on the ground. He saw a tiny crocus poking through the soft dirt.

And he was glad.

The baby sheep looked between two rocks. He saw a big, green woolly worm peeking out of the crack.
And he was glad.

The baby sheep walked on down a rocky hillside. He stopped. He looked back up the hill. Where was his grassy, hill home? Where was his warm, woolly mother?

Then the baby sheep saw a sparrow sitting on a twig of a prickly bush. He asked the bird, "Can you help me find my way home? I want my grassy, hill home. I need my warm, woolly mother."

The sparrow said to the baby sheep, "Don't
worry, the good shepherd will find you and take
you safely home."

Walking on, the baby sheep saw a lily growing among the grass. He asked the tall, slender flower, "Can you help me find my way home? I want my grassy, hill home. I need my warm, woolly mother."

The lily said to the baby sheep, "Don't worry,
the good shepherd will find you and take you
safely home."

As he walked on, the baby sheep saw a badger climbing over some rocks. He asked the small, furry animal, "Can you help me find my way home? I want my grassy, hill home. I need my warm, woolly mother."

The badger said to the baby sheep, "Don't worry, the good shepherd will find you and take you safely home."

But the baby sheep was now so tired, he lay down against a rock and began to cry. He was all alone and afraid. Who could take him safely home?

Then the baby sheep heard something. He stopped crying and lifted his head. Someone was calling to him.

"Come to me, little one," said the good shepherd. "I will take you safely home again."

The baby sheep ran to the shepherd. And the good shepherd gently lifted the baby sheep into his strong arms. He carried the baby sheep to his grassy, hill home. He was safely home again with his warm, woolly mother. And he was glad.

33

"There he is, Mama! I see him! I see Jesus!"
Snatching his hand from his mother, the young boy
darted up the path.

"Come back here! Stay with us." Laughing, Mama turned to her daughter. "Run and catch up with your brother so he doesn't get into trouble."

Jesus had come to their town, and everyone was excited to see him! A crowd was already gathering to hear him speak.

Mama and Papa hurried to catch up to their children. As they got close to the crowd, they saw their children running toward a group of men.

Jesus was behind the men and the children were having a hard time getting through.

"Hold on," a big man said angrily, stepping quickly in front of the children. "Leave Jesus alone! Don't bother him."

Tears filled the boy's eyes. Gently taking her brother's hand, the little girl quietly spoke. "Please, sir, we just want to see Jesus. We won't bother him."

By that time, Papa caught up to his children. Out of breath, he hurriedly said, "We just want Jesus to bless our children."

Other families crowded close. "Us too," one mother said. "Can Jesus bless our children too?"

Shocked at the boldness of these people,
the man responded, "Jesus can't be bothered.
Go away!"

Without another word to the families around them, the men turned their attention back to Jesus. They stood close to him, protecting him from the crowd.

Seeing that nothing else could be done, Papa hugged his little boy close and the family sadly turned to leave.

The family hadn't gone far when they heard a voice call out, "Wait!"

They turned around. It was Jesus! He was calling them! Maybe the men were wrong and Jesus really didn't mind if they brought their children to him. The little boy was so excited!

"Let the children come to me," Jesus said. "Don't stop them! For the kingdom of God belongs to such as these. I assure you, anyone who doesn't have their kind of faith will never get into the kingdom of God."

The men stepped aside so the families could get closer to Jesus. As they moved, the young boy's face lit up. His feet danced in delight. Finally he could see Jesus and get close enough to touch him!

Squealing with joy, the little boy ran
toward Jesus, throwing himself into
Jesus' open arms.

Other children followed right behind the boy, each receiving a hug and gentle touch from Jesus. Looking into each smiling face, Jesus blessed them. Joy shone in the eyes of the children. They knew they were special. Jesus loved them all very much.

Peter loved to fish. One day Jesus said to Peter, "Come, follow me."

So Peter left his fishing boat and became a disciple, or follower, of Jesus. Peter and the other disciples traveled with Jesus as he taught and helped and loved the people.

Peter saw Jesus do great things only Jesus could do.
Peter was there when Jesus fed 5,000 men with just five
loaves and two fish.

Peter was there when Jesus walked on the
water of a stormy lake.

90

Peter was with Jesus before Jesus died.

And three days later, Peter and John saw an empty tomb. Jesus had risen from the dead!

A few days later, Jesus asked Peter, "Do you love me?"
Peter said yes!

Then Jesus said, "Feed my lambs." Peter knew that when Jesus said "my lambs," he was talking about people who needed to know and follow Jesus. Peter needed to obey and tell others about Jesus.

So Peter went to Jerusalem and preached to a great crowd of all kinds of people.

Peter said, "Everyone who follows Jesus will be saved."

Peter went to the temple in Jerusalem too. He helped a man who could not walk, and he told even more people about Jesus. Peter preached, "Stop doing wrong. Turn to God."

More and more people wanted to hear about Jesus.
But some of the leaders became angry. They told Peter
and the other disciples to stop talking about Jesus. The
leaders even put Peter and the other disciples in jail!

But during the night, an angel from God opened the jail doors. The angel told the disciples to go tell about Jesus. And they did!

The leaders were angry again, but Peter said, "We must obey God." Peter kept telling people about Jesus. Many people listened to Peter. They wanted to follow Jesus.

Peter taught the people more about Jesus. The people
learned to pray, to love one another, and to praise God.

Jesus asked Peter, "Do you love me?"
And Peter said yes!

Paul and Silas loved God very much. They traveled to many different cities, teaching about Jesus and saying that he was the Son of God.

It was the same when they came to Philippi. Only this time, things turned out differently.

Everything was fine the first few days. Then Paul cast out an evil spirit in Jesus' name. This made some men really angry.

The angry men had Paul and Silas arrested, beaten, and thrown into my jail.

I put them inside their cell. They were dangerous men, and I had to be careful.

If they escaped, I would be blamed, so I checked twice to make sure their hands and feet were firmly chained.

Everything was very quiet . . . until right around midnight. That's when I heard something strange. I crept through the dark halls of the jail, looking and listening.

It was Paul and Silas! They were in their cell, chained up tight, singing at the top of their lungs. And they were happy! I had never seen anything like this before. They sat singing and praying while the other prisoners leaned in close to listen. They had to be crazy!

Suddenly, the ground began to shake. My legs wobbled under me. All around, I could hear walls crumbling and metal crashing.

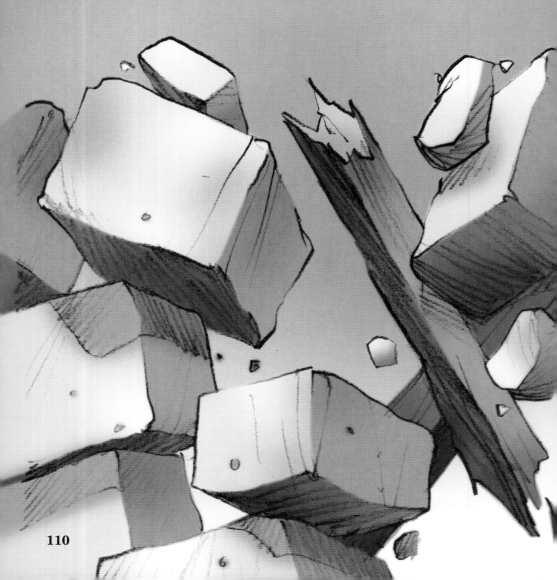

Then my feet flew out from under me! I was terrified!

Finally, it stopped. I looked around at the crumbled jail. What a mess! Going inside a cell, I saw loose chains lying all over the floor. Where were Paul and Silas? Were the other prisoners gone? What was I going to do? My life was ruined!

As I picked up my sword to end my life, a voice stopped me. "Don't harm yourself! We're all here!"

Quickly, I dropped the chains and looked around to see who had spoken.

It was Paul. I couldn't believe it! He was right. Every prisoner was still there. No one had left the crumbled jail after the earthquake.

That's when I knew Paul and Silas were men of God. These things that happened—the singing, the earthquake, the prisoners not escaping—they were truly amazing. I wanted to know this powerful God they served.

"How can I be saved?" I asked, kneeling in front of them. They told me to believe in the Lord Jesus Christ and I would be saved. From that point on, I believed.

I took Paul and Silas to my home where I washed their wounds. Then I asked them to baptize me, and everyone in my family. What a wonderful experience! Jesus was my Savior! Joy filled my heart and I felt like singing. My life was changed. This jailer was set free!

Slap, slap, slap. Saul's sandals slapped a rhythm on the road. He was on his way to Damascus to stop the Christians there from following Jesus.

Suddenly a bright light flashed in the sky and Saul was blinded. Saul fell to the ground. A voice said, "Saul, Saul, why are you hurting me?"

"Who are you?" Saul asked the voice. It was Jesus!

Led by his friends, Saul stumbled into the city.

Jesus told a man named Ananias to go to Saul. Ananias was afraid, but because he served Jesus, Ananias went anyway. Through God's power, Ananias healed Saul's eyes and helped Saul learn more about Jesus.

Now Saul loved Jesus. Saul wanted to please Jesus and be like him. Soon Saul became known to people as *Paul*.

121

Walk, walk, walk. Paul strode along the road once again. He traveled from city to city preaching the good news about Jesus. Paul told how Jesus had forgiven and changed him.

Many people who heard Paul's words became
Christians. Wherever Paul went, churches began to grow.

In some towns, however, Paul's message made people angry. They accused Paul of stirring up trouble. The leaders in the town of Philippi decided to do something to stop Paul.

Scratch, scratch, scratch. Paul's feet scraped the floor as he was dragged through the door of a jailhouse!

Even though he was beaten and put in chains, Paul would not stop preaching and praising God.

Paul kept on walking from city to city. Paul preached,
"Have faith in Jesus and your sins will be forgiven" and
"You can live the right way with Jesus' help."

More churches began. But once again, some people became angry at Paul's words. One night, Paul made a narrow escape from the people who wanted to kill him! *Clop, clop, clop.* Horses' hooves quickly carried Paul away from the city of Jerusalem.

Paul's enemies—the people who hated to hear about Jesus—made more and more trouble for Paul. They did not want to change their wrong ways. The Roman officials did not know what to do about Paul. They arrested him.

Paul made another long trip. *Thunk, thunk, thunk.* Paul climbed the gangplank of a wooden ship headed to Rome.

Now a prisoner, Paul was unable to travel to the churches growing in faraway cities. But Paul still would not—*could* not—stop telling about Jesus.

Crunch, crunch, crunch. The feet that kicked up dust and gravel now belonged to a messenger. He was coming to get letters written by Paul to the churches.

We can read Paul's letters today! They make up a large part of the New Testament in the Bible.

Paul's letters say, "Be kind and compassionate to one another, forgiving each other, just as in Christ God forgave you" (Ephesians 4:32). "Stand firm in the faith; . . . be strong. Do everything in love" (1 Corinthians 16:13, 14).

Paul's letters can help us be better followers of Jesus. Now *we* can go and tell about Jesus. *Walk, walk, walk!*